T0387169

TYRANNOSAURUS REX

by Laura K. Murray

Consultant: Mathew J. Wedel, PhD
Western University of Health Sciences
Pomona, California

PEBBLE
a capstone imprint

Published by Pebble, an imprint of Capstone
1710 Roe Crest Drive, North Mankato, Minnesota 56003
capstonepub.com

Library of Congress Cataloging-in-Publication Data
Names: Murray, Laura K., 1989– author.
Title: Tyrannosaurus rex / by Laura K. Murray.
Description: North Mankato, Minnesota : Pebble, an imprint of Capstone, [2025] | Series: Dinosaur guides | Includes bibliographical references. | Audience: Ages 5–8 | Audience: Grades 2–3 | Summary: "What do readers want to know about Tyrannosaurus rex? Everything! Engaging text and images make this book a great choice for information to use in a report or just to read for fun"—Provided by publisher.
Identifiers: LCCN 2024022997 (print) | LCCN 2024022998 (ebook) | ISBN 9780756589141 (hardcover) | ISBN 9780756589363 (paperback) | ISBN 9780756589189 (pdf) | ISBN 9780756589387 (kindle edition) | ISBN 9780756589370 (epub)
Subjects: LCSH: Tyrannosaurus rex—Juvenile literature.
Classification: LCC QE862.S3 M887 2025 (print) | LCC QE862.S3 (ebook) | DDC 567.912/9—dc23/eng/20240524
LC record available at https://lccn.loc.gov/2024022997
LC ebook record available at https://lccn.loc.gov/2024022998

Editorial Credits
Editor: Erika L. Shores; Designer: Dina Her; Media Researcher: Jo Miller; Production Specialist: Tori Abraham

Image Credits
Alamy: Sueddeutsche Zeitung Photo, 26; Capstone: Jon Hughes, cover, 4, 5, 6, 9, 10, 13, 15, 16, 19, 22; Dreamstime: Petr Svec, 21; Getty Images: BART MAAT, 28, Mark Wilson, 27, The Washington Post, 25; Science Source: Esther van Hulsen/Stocktrek Images, 20; Shutterstock: Kues, background (throughout), Warpaint, 1, 12

Printed and bound in China. 6098

Table of Contents

Words in **bold** are in the glossary.

King of the Dinosaurs

What huge dinosaur was one of the most feared hunters ever? Tyrannosaurus rex! Its name means "king of the **tyrant** lizards." It is called T. rex for short.

T. rex was one of the biggest meat-eating animals on land. It was about the length of a school bus. It walked on two legs. T. rex lived during the Late Cretaceous Period. That was 68 to 66 million years ago. T. rex was one of the last dinosaurs to walk on Earth.

Where in the World

T. rex lived in the western United States and Canada. In the U.S., it roamed Montana, Wyoming, South Dakota, New Mexico, and Texas. In Canada, scientists found T. rex **fossils** in Alberta and Saskatchewan.

North America looked very different when T. rex lived. The **continent** was split into two pieces of land. A deep sea flowed between them.

Tyrannosaurus rex hunted in forests and river valleys. Today, those same areas are dry and grassy. But the land was different millions of years ago. It was like a floodplain. That is an area near a river.

Back then, the land was rich with plants and wildlife. Mammals, birds, insects, and other animals made their homes there. Temperatures were warmer.

9

Did You Know?

There were other huge dinosaurs. But they lived during different times. Giganotosaurus was about the same size as T. rex. It lived 30 million years before T. rex.

Tyrannosaurus Rex Bodies

T. rex was a giant **predator**. It stood 12 feet (3.7 meters) tall. It may have been more than 40 feet (12.2 m) long. It was heavy too! It weighed between 11,000 and 19,800 pounds (5,000 and 9,000 kilograms).

T. rex had short arms for its big body. They were only 3 feet (0.9 m) long. This would be like a 6-foot (183-centimeter) human having 5-inch (12.7-cm) arms!

T. rex is known for its large head.
Its skull was up to 5 feet (1.5 m) long.
A big, heavy tail helped T. rex
stay balanced.

Did You Know?

A T. rex bite was so powerful it could have crushed a car. T. rex crunched through bones.

T. rex had 60 teeth. They were pointy and sharp. Each tooth was 8 inches (20 cm) long. The teeth could stab into **prey**. That kept the prey from escaping.

What Tyrannosaurus Rex Ate

T. rex was a meat eater. It ate other animals. It was so big that it could eat anything it wanted. It ate other dinosaurs. It may have eaten other T. rexes too.

T. rex was an apex predator. That means no other animals hunted it. It was at the top of the **food chain**. T. rex was also a scavenger. It ate animals that were already dead.

T. rex could not run very fast. It took a lot of work to move its big body. Scientists believe it may have walked 10 to 15 miles (16 to 24 kilometers) per hour. But it did not have to be fast to catch its prey. Its big stride helped.

T. rex had sharp senses. They helped it hunt down its food. T. rex had a very good sense of smell. It likely had good eyesight too. Its eyes faced forward like a wolf's.

T. rex used its jaw to throw its prey into the air. It caught the food in its mouth. T. rex had large blood vessels on top of its head. They kept its brain cool while it ate.

Scientists still do not know why T. rex had such tiny arms. Some believe their short arms may have helped when scavenging. If several T. rexes were eating a dead animal, their arms would not get in the way.

Life of Tyrannosaurus Rex

Like all dinosaurs, T. rex hatched from an egg. Some scientists think T. rex was covered in feathers when it hatched. It grew quickly. It may have grown by about 1,500 pounds (680 kg) per year. It likely reached its full size as a teenager.

Did You Know?

It took 10 years just to dig out the bones of Scotty. It took about another 20 years to put them together and study them.

The oldest T. rex found lived to at least 28 years old. Scientists discovered the fossil in 1991 in Saskatchewan, Canada. They named the skeleton Scotty.

Scientists study fossils to learn about how T. rex ate, lived, and died. They study bite marks on bones. They have even found fossils of T. rex poop.

Scientists do not know if T. rexes lived together. They have not found groups of T. rex fossils. They think T. rexes fought each other over food or **mates**. Some scientists now believe T. rexes may have hunted in packs like wolves.

In 1988, fossil hunter Kathy Wankel discovered a nearly complete T. rex fossil. It was in Montana. Scientists think this T. rex was about 18 years old when it died. It may have weighed between 12,000 and 14,000 pounds (5,400 and 6,400 kg).

The T. rex had been sick and injured during its life. Scientists could not tell if it was male or female. But they could tell that the dinosaur died near a riverbed.

the Wankel T. rex

Discovering Tyrannosaurus Rex

In 1902, scientist Barnum Brown discovered the first T. rex fossil. It was part of a skeleton. He found it in Montana. In 1905, H. F. Osborn named the dinosaur.

Barnum Brown studying dinosaur fossils.

Sue

In 1990, fossil hunter Sue Hendrickson made an important find. She found T. rex bones in South Dakota. The skeleton was even more complete than the Wankel T. rex. It was later named Sue.

T. rex is one of the most famous dinosaurs. It is featured in movies, books, and toys. But there are still many things people do not know about T. rex.

Scientists ask questions about Tyrannosaurus rex. They study fossils. They look for clues in footprints, bones, and more. They use X-rays, **laser** scans, and computer models. There is much more to learn about this amazing, fearsome dinosaur!

Fast Facts

Name: Tyrannosaurus rex (meaning "king of the tyrant lizards")

Lived: Late Cretaceous period (about 68 to 66 million years ago)

Range: western United States (Montana, Wyoming, South Dakota, New Mexico, Texas) and Canada (Alberta, Saskatchewan)

Habitat: forests and river valleys

Food: other animals and dinosaurs; animal remains

Threats: none

Discovered: 1902, Montana

Glossary

continent (KON-tuh-nuht)—one of Earth's seven large land masses

food chain (FOOD CHAYN)—a series of living things in which each uses the next usually lower member of the series as a food source

fossil (FAH-suhl)—the remains or traces of a living thing from many years ago

laser (LAY-zur)—a tool that uses powerful light

mate (MAYT)—a partner that joins with another to produce young

predator (PRED-uh-tur)—an animal that hunts other animals for food

prey (PRAY)—an animal that is hunted or killed by another animal for food

tyrant (TYE-rant)—a ruler who is cruel and unfair

Read More

Nelson, Louise. *Creatures of the Cretaceous.* Minneapolis: Bearport Publishing, 2023.

Throp, Claire. *Read All About Dinosaurs.* North Mankato, MN: Capstone, 2022.

Vonder Brink, Tracy. *The Tyrannosaurus Rex.* New York: Crabtree Publishing, 2024.

Internet Sites

American Museum of Natural History: Tyrannosaurus rex
amnh.org/dinosaurs/tyrannosaurus-rex

National Geographic Kids: Tyrannosaurus rex
kids.nationalgeographic.com/animals/prehistoric/facts/tyrannosaurus-rex

University of California at Berkeley: The Tyrant Lizards: The Tyrannosauridae
ucmp.berkeley.edu/diapsids/saurischia/tyrannosauridae.html

Index

About the Author

Laura K. Murray is the Minnesota-based author of more than 100 books for young readers. She loves learning from fellow readers and helping others find their reading superpowers! Visit LauraKMurray.com.